CHAT GPT IN OUR DAYS

A Book Written By Chat GPT

Kimoy Fearon

TABLE OF CONTENT

Chapter 5: Chat GPT's Impact on Different Sectors

- Business and commerce

- Healthcare

- Education

- Entertainment and media

- Government and politics

Chapter 6: The Future of Chat GPT

- Predictions for future advancements and capabilities

- Potential future uses and applications of Chat GPT

- Discussion on ethical considerations and regulations for the use of Chat GPT technology

Chapter 7: Conclusion

- Summary of key points and takeaways

- Final thoughts on the impact and significance of Chat GPT in our lives.

Glossary and Terms

DISCLAIMER

This book is intended to provide an overview of Chat GPT technology and its impact on various industries and aspects of society. The information contained in this book is based on research and available sources and is accurate as of the knowledge cutoff date. However, due to the rapidly changing nature of this field, some information may have become outdated or superseded. Readers are encouraged to conduct their research and seek additional resources to stay informed of the latest developments in this area. The opinions and viewpoints expressed in this book are solely those of the author and do not reflect the views of any organization or entity. The author and publisher are not responsible for any errors or omissions and do not guarantee the accuracy of the information contained in this book.

INTRODUCTION

Do you know how long it took Chat GPT to accumulate (1M) One Million subscribers? One Week! That's right, Chat GPT unlike other major global tech companies has garnered 1M users in just (5) five days after its launch in November 2022, while Instagram took more than two months, and Facebook after its launch in February 2004 took ten months. So what makes Chat GPT so fascinatingly interesting?

Chat GPT is a cutting-edge technology that has transformed natural language processing. Chat GPT models, which are based on machine learning algorithms and deep neural networks, can understand and generate human-like text with unprecedented accuracy and fluency. This has significantly impacted a wide range of industries and applications, including customer service and education, as well as entertainment and media.

However, the development and use of Chat GPT, like any new technology, raises important ethical concerns, such as privacy and security, the potential for bias and discrimination, and the impact on employment.

This book will look at the history and development of Chat GPT technology, as well as its current capabilities and applications, and the impact it has on various industries and aspects of our lives. It will also investigate the ethical implications and regulations surrounding its use, as well as forecast future advancements and capabilities. Readers will have a thorough understanding of the impact and significance of Chat GPT in our lives and the world at large by the end of this book.

CHAPTER 1

What is Chat GPT?

Definition Of Chat Gpt And Its Purpose

Chat GPT is an artificial intelligence language model developed by OpenAI that can generate human-like text based on the input it receives. Its goal is to improve human-computer contact and communication by creating text that looks and sounds like a human response. Chat GPT is used in a variety of applications like customer assistance, education, and entertainment.

A Brief History of the Development of Chat GPT Technology

With the growth of deep learning and natural language processing in the early 2010s, the development of Chat GPT technology began. In 2018, OpenAI, an artificial intelligence research group, released its first GPT (Generative Pretrained Transformer) model. This was a game-changing breakthrough in the field of language models since it was the first time a model was trained on a big corpus of text and could create coherent and varied content.

OpenAI has since continued to develop and refine GPT technology, releasing GPT-2 in 2019 and GPT-3 in 2020. These models were trained on a wider corpus of literature, resulting in even more powerful language production capabilities. Chat GPT has gained popularity due to its human-like text production.

Explanation Of How Chat GPT Works And How It's Different from Traditional Language Models

Chat GPT works by using a deep neural network called a transformer to generate text based on the input it receives. The model has been trained on a large corpus of text, allowing it to generate text that resembles human writing in terms of style, tone, and content.

When Chat GPT receives an input, it uses the context of that input to generate a response. The response is generated based on the probabilities of the words that come after the input, as learned from the training corpus. The generated response is then fed back into the model as the new input, allowing Chat GPT to generate multiple rounds of text in a conversation-like manner.

In various respects, Chat GPT differs from typical language models. For starters, it has significantly more data on which to learn, allowing it to create much more diversified and coherent content. Second, unlike standard recurrent neural network-based language models, Chat GPT has a transformer-based design. This enables it to manage long-term dependencies more effectively and create more contextually aware language.

In essence, Chat GPT is a cutting-edge language model that generates human-like text depending on the input it receives using deep learning techniques. Its innovative design and extensive training corpus make it a versatile tool with many uses.

CHAPTER 2

Development of Chat GPT over Time

Early Beginnings of Chat GPT Technology

The origins of Chat GPT technology may be traced back to the early 2010s, with the emergence of deep learning and natural language processing. At the time, academics and technologists were working on language models capable of producing human-like text.

OpenAI, an artificial intelligence research group, was one of the early pioneers in this subject. In 2018, OpenAI released its first GPT (Generative Pretrained Transformer) model, marking a significant step forward in the development of language models.

In comparison to subsequent models, the early GPT models were trained on a very tiny corpus of text. Nonetheless, they revealed considerable advances in language models' capacity to create human-like prose. These early prototypes laid the path for future growth and advancement in the field of Chat GPT technology.

Key Milestones and Advancements in Chat GPT Technology

Here are some of the significant milestones and achievements in Chat GPT technology development:

1. GPT-1 (2018): OpenAI released the first GPT model, signifying a massive step forward in the development of language models.

2. GPT-2 (2019): OpenAI published GPT-2, a more sophisticated and broader version of its language model. GPT-2 was trained on a significantly wider corpus of material, allowing it to create more diversified and cohesive content that is more diversified and cohesive.

3. GPT-3 (2020): In 2020, OpenAI will release GPT-3, its biggest language model yet. GPT-3 displayed impressive language-generating skills, including the capacity to execute tasks such as translation and summarization, thanks to its powerful transformer-based architecture and enormous training corpus.

4. Transfer Learning for NLP (2020): Advances in transfer learning in natural language processing have allowed large language models such as GPT-3 to be fine-tuned on smaller, domain-specific datasets, allowing for more focused and specialized language creation.

5. Integration with Other Technologies (from 2021 to the present): The integration of Chat GPT with other technologies as virtual assistants and conversational AI has opened up new avenues for human-computer interaction and communication. These key milestones and advancements have continued to push the boundaries of what is possible with Chat GPT technology and have paved the way for further developments in the future.

Comparison of Early Chat GPT Models to Current Models and Their Capabilities

Early Chat GPT models, like as GPT-1, marked a substantial advancement in language models' capacity to create human-like text. They were, however, restricted in their capabilities when compared to modern versions.

The size of the models is a significant difference. Early Chat GPT models, such as GPT-1, were trained on a much smaller corpus of text than contemporary models, like as GPT-3. This means that modern models have a considerably bigger and more diversified spectrum of information to pull from when creating text, resulting in more coherent and diverse outputs.

Another distinction is the model architecture. Early Chat GPT models relied on a simple recurrent neural network design, but contemporary versions rely on a transformer-based architecture. This enables existing models to better manage long-term dependencies and provide more contextually aware language.

In terms of capabilities, early Chat GPT models were largely used for text synthesis and language translation, but modern models, such as GPT-3, can perform a broader variety of activities, including question-answering, summarization, and even code development.

Overall, advances in Chat GPT technology have resulted in much bigger and more complex machines with a broader variety of functions throughout the years.

CHAPTER 3

Benefits of Chat GPT

Improved Communication and Accessibility

Chat GPT technology's integration with conversational AI and virtual assistants is one of the primary ways it has increased communication and accessibility.

Chat GPT has made it simpler for individuals to get information and conduct things without the requirement of specialist technical skills by enabling natural language engagement with technology. Chat GPT-powered virtual assistants, for example, may assist consumers with everyday chores such as arranging appointments, ordering food, and checking the weather.

Chat GPT has also helped communication in other ways, such as the creation of language models capable of producing human-like prose in numerous languages. This has made it simpler for individuals to speak across language boundaries, enhancing accessibility and fostering greater understanding among people from many nations and cultures.

Finally, Chat GPT has made it easier for those with impairments to communicate. Chat GPT-powered virtual assistants, for example, can relate to assistive technology to give an alternative mode of communication for those who cannot utilize traditional input methods. The advancements in Chat GPT technology have improved communication and accessibility in a variety of ways, making it easier for people to access information and communicate with each other.

Enhanced Customer Service and Support

Chat GPT technology has dramatically changed customer care and support by allowing businesses to communicate with consumers in more efficient and productive ways.

Conversational AI and virtual assistants driven by Chat GPT are one powerful strategy by which this was accomplished. Customers may use natural language to connect with businesses, making it easier for them to receive the information they need and handle concerns promptly. This has resulted in higher customer satisfaction and shorter response times.

Chat GPT has also been used to construct more powerful chatbots that can perform a broader range of customer care and support functions, such as addressing client inquiries, delivering product information, and processing refunds, in addition to conversational AI. As a result, customer service and support operations have become more efficient and scalable.

Ultimately, the use of Chat GPT technology in customer care and support has given organizations new and improved methods to communicate with consumers, resulting in increased customer happiness and efficiency.

Streamlining Of Business Processes

Chat GPT technology has the potential to improve a wide range of corporate processes, including customer care and support, as well as internal operations and management.

Conversational AI and virtual assistants, which may automate regular activities like answering consumer inquiries, delivering product information, and processing orders, are one method Chat

GPT might optimize company operations. Businesses may then divert their resources to higher-value jobs, improving overall efficiency.

Chat GPT may also be used to automate internal corporate activities like data input and report production. Chat GPT can assist by simplifying these activities by employing natural language processing and text creation capabilities, decreasing the time and resources necessary to execute them.

Finally, Chat GPT may aid enterprises in decision-making and strategy planning by providing insights and analysis gained from massive amounts of data. This can help businesses make more informed decisions. faster and much more effectively, resulting in enhanced operations and overall performance.

Consequently, the application of Chat GPT technology has the potential to increase the efficiency and productivity of a wide range of company activities, from customer care and assistance to

internal operations and management.

Advancements In the Fields of Education and Healthcare

Chat GPT technological improvements have had a huge influence on both the realm of education and the healthcare business.

Chat GPT technology has been utilized in education to create virtual tutors and educational assistants that may aid students with their studies by offering tailored feedback and assistance. This has the potential to increase access to education and improve students' learning experiences.

Chat GPT technology has been utilized in healthcare to create virtual health assistants that may help patients manage their health by offering information, reminders, and personalized advice. This has the potential to enhance patient outcomes while also lowering the strain on healthcare professionals.

Furthermore, Chat GPT has been utilized to create language

models that may aid healthcare practitioners with activities like illness diagnosis and treatment, medical picture analysis, and patient report generation. This has the potential to increase healthcare process accuracy and efficiency, resulting in better patient outcomes.

CHAPTER 4

Drawbacks of Chat GPT

Bias and Discrimination in Language Generation

Bias and prejudice might be issues while developing and using Chat GPT language models. This is because these models are trained on massive volumes of text data that may contain biases and discriminatory wording. As a result, the created outputs may reflect these prejudices, potentially leading to prejudice and the perpetuating of negative stereotypes.

Gender and racial biases, for example, have been discovered in language generation models, where they may provide outputs that support gender and racial preconceptions. Similarly, models trained on biased data may create outputs that discriminate against certain categories of people, such as persons with impairments or individuals from specific ethnicities or origins.

To address these concerns, developers, and organizations must detect and minimize bias in the data used to train these algorithms. This might entail a variety of data sources being used. Approaches such as data augmentation and bias correction are being used, and regular monitoring and testing models for bias.

Furthermore, companies must have explicit rules and standards in place for the creation and deployment of Chat GPT models to guarantee that they are utilized ethically and responsibly and do not propagate detrimental prejudices and discrimination.

Threat To Privacy and Security

Chat GPT technology is built on machine learning algorithms and Natural Language Processing (NLP) approaches, allowing it to create human-like text from incoming data. The possible uses and applications of Chat GPT are expanding as technology advances, but it's crucial to be mindful of the potential threats to privacy and security that arise with the usage of these models.

One source of worry is the collecting and storage of personal data, as Chat GPT models need access to enormous volumes of text data that may contain sensitive information about persons. This information must be securely maintained and safeguarded against unauthorized access, misuse, or theft.

Another cause for concern is the possibility of malevolent use of Chat GPT models, such as the transmission of false news or disinformation. These models are capable of producing human-like writing that may be used to deceive and influence individuals and organizations with catastrophic repercussions.

Furthermore, Chat GPT models may be used to automate specific forms of cyber-attacks, like phishing or spam, which pose a danger to privacy and security while also having broader societal and economic implications.

To tackle these issues, firms must install robust security measures such as encryption and access restrictions, as well as perform regular security audits to guarantee sensitive data is protected.

Moreover, organizations should be aware of the potential for malicious use of Chat GPT models and take steps to prevent and mitigate these risks, such as monitoring and detecting suspicious activity, employing verification techniques, and educating users about the potential risks associated with their use.

Overall, while Chat GPT technology has the potential to

significantly improve communication and accessibility, it is critical to be aware of possible privacy and security vulnerabilities and to take efforts to address and minimize these dangers.

Dependence On Technology and Potential Job Loss

When analyzing the influence of Chat GPT technology, another factor to examine is its ability to displace human labor and cause job loss.

As Chat GPT models improve and become more proficient, they will be able to undertake a broader range of functions traditionally performed by human labor, including customer support, content production, and data analysis.

This move toward automation and artificial intelligence (AI) may result in major job losses as businesses strive to decrease costs and boost efficiency by replacing human labor with technology.

Nevertheless, as people become increasingly reliant on Chat GPT technology for daily jobs and activities, there is a fear that they may become overly dependent on technology, resulting in a loss of vital skills and expertise.

Organizations must examine and execute retraining programs for individuals who may be displaced by the global trend toward automation and AI to address this possible impact on employment. This might involve assisting people in developing new skills, transitioning into new jobs, and exploring alternative models for work and employment in the age of AI and automation.

In addition, individuals can take steps to prepare for the future of work, by continually learning and developing new skills, and seeking to stay up to date with the latest developments in technology and innovation.

All in all, while Chat GPT technology has the potential to greatly improve communication and accessibility, it is critical to consider and address the potential impact on employment and work, as well as to find ways to support workers and individuals as they transition to a more technologically-driven future.

CHAPTER 5

Chat GPT's Impact on Different Sectors

Challenges in Regulating and Controlling Its Use

Because of the fast growth of Chat GPT technology, legislators and regulators have considerable challenges in regulating and managing its usage.

One of the most challenging hurdles is ensuring that Chat GPT models are used ethically and responsibly, notably in areas of prejudice and discrimination, privacy protection, and stopping the spread of disinformation and hate speech.

Another difficulty is the quick rate of technological development and innovation, which makes it difficult for regulators to stay up and create adequate rules to manage the possible hazards and implications of Chat GPT technology.

Furthermore, there are issues in ensuring that Chat GPT technology is utilized publicly and responsibly, particularly when it comes to the decision-making procedures and algorithms employed by these models.

To overcome these issues, governments and regulators must collaborate with technology firms, professionals, and civil society organizations to create clear and effective laws for Chat GPT technology usage. This may involve the establishment of standards for the responsible use of these models, as well as the creation of oversight systems to guarantee that these criteria are met.

Therefore, greater openness and accountability are required in the creation and deployment of Chat GPT models, particularly in their decision-making procedures and algorithms. This can include strategies like explainability and interpretability, which help users and regulators understand how these models make decisions and function.

Consequently, although the use of Chat GPT technology brings great prospects and advantages, it also raises substantial regulatory and control concerns that must be addressed to guarantee that this technology is utilized responsibly, ethically, and safely.

Business And Commerce

Chat GPT technology has had a huge influence on business and commerce, transforming how firms engage with their consumers and function.

One of the most significant ways that Chat GPT technology has altered business and commerce is through chatbots, which enable businesses to give automated customer assistance and support 24 hours a day, seven days a week. This has substantially enhanced customer service efficiency and accessibility, making it simpler for clients to acquire answers to their inquiries and fix their difficulties.

Furthermore, Chat GPT models are being utilized in a range of other business and commerce applications, including as content production, data analysis, and market research. These models can analyze massive volumes of data fast and correctly, producing insights and suggestions that may help businesses make better decisions and increase operational efficiency.

Another significant influence of Chat GPT technology on business and commerce is the way it has changed the way businesses connect with their consumers. Companies can now communicate with their consumers in a more customized and human-like manner thanks to the emergence of chatbots and conversational interfaces, which have increased customer happiness and loyalty.

Chat GPT technology has had a dramatic influence on business and commerce, substantially improving the efficiency, accessibility, and consumer involvement of businesses across a wide range of sectors. As this technology advances and evolves, it is likely to have an even bigger influence on how businesses function and engage with their consumers in the future.

Healthcare

Chat GPT technology has also had a big influence on the world of healthcare, with the potential to redefine how healthcare is given and accessed.

One of the primary applications of Chat GPT technology in healthcare is the development of chatbots and virtual health assistants, which provide patients with quick and convenient access to health information and advice. These chatbots may give information on a wide range of health issues, from symptoms and diagnosis to treatment and management, and can assist patients in making health-related decisions.

Furthermore, Chat GPT models are utilized in a range of other healthcare applications, including medical research and drug discovery, where they can analyze massive volumes of data and offer insights and predictions that can improve medical decision-making.

Another significant outcome of Chat GPT technology in healthcare is how it has changed the way healthcare practitioners engage with their patients. Healthcare providers may now contact patients more quickly and deliver more tailored and accessible treatment thanks to the advent of telemedicine and remote consultations.

Thus, Chat GPT technology has had a significant influence on healthcare and has the potential to dramatically enhance the accessibility, quality, and cost of healthcare for individuals all across the world. As this technology advances and evolves, it is expected to have an even bigger influence on the way healthcare is provided and received.

Education

Chat GPT technology has also had a tremendous impact on education, with the potential to transform the way knowledge is presented and consumed.

One of the primary applications of Chat GPT technology in the classroom is the creation of chatbots and virtual instructors, which offer students with quick access to knowledge and help while they study. These chatbots may answer questions on a variety of topics, offer feedback on assignments and exams, and assist students in staying on track with their studies.

Secondly, Chat GPT models are utilized in a range of other educational applications, including language learning and evaluation, where they may analyze student performance and give individualized feedback and suggestions.

Another noticeable effect of Chat GPT technology in education is how it has changed the way teachers communicate with their pupils. Teachers may now interact with students more quickly and deliver more tailored and accessible training thanks to the advent of online learning and remote teaching.

Chat GPT technology is revolutionizing education by increasing access, quality, and efficacy. So far, the impact has been substantial, and it is expected to grow as tech advances.

Entertainment and media

Chat GPT technology has also had a tremendous influence on the sectors of entertainment and media, with the potential to transform the way content is generated and consumed.

One of the primary applications of Chat GPT technology in entertainment and media is the creation of chatbots and virtual assistants, which allow consumers fast access to information and suggestions on movies, TV programs, music, books, and other types of entertainment. These chatbots may assess users' preferences and make customized suggestions, assisting users in discovering new material that they're likely to enjoy.

Additionally, Chat GPT models are being utilized in a range of other entertainment and media applications, including content generation, where they can produce screenplays, narratives, and characters for use in movies, TV shows, and video games.

Another important impact of Chat GPT technology in entertainment and media is how it has changed the way material is consumed. Users may now access and enjoy the information in new and more convenient ways thanks to the emergence of voice-activated devices and conversational interfaces.

Overall, Chat GPT technology has had a major influence on entertainment and media, with the ability to substantially improve user experience and provide new options for content creators. As this technology advances and evolves, it is expected to have an even bigger influence on the way media is produced and consumed.

Government and Politics

Chatbots and virtual assistants powered by Chat GPT technology are changing the way citizens access government information and assistance. These chatbots can answer questions on taxes, voting, and benefits, making it simpler for individuals to grasp government processes. Chat GPT models may also be used to help with policy analysis and decision-making by assessing data and giving suggestions. As internet platforms and mobile devices provide a quicker connection with representatives, technology has revolutionized how individuals interact with the government. Overall, Chat GPT is having a huge influence on government and politics by enhancing efficiency and citizen involvement.

CHAPTER 6

The Future of Chat GPT

Predictions for future advancements and capabilities

1. Chat GPT technology is projected to evolve and become more complex soon, introducing new features and uses. The following are a few prominent forecasts regarding future developments and capabilities:

2. Increased personalization: Chat GPT models will be able to comprehend and respond to individual users more accurately, giving individualized experiences and suggestions.

3. Better language generation: Chat GPT models will be able to create more realistic and human-like language, allowing users to connect with them more easily.

4. Better conversation management: Chat GPT models will be able to handle many conversations simultaneously and offer context-aware responses, making them more useful for customer service and support applications.

5. Greater interaction with other technologies: Chat GPT models will become increasingly integrated with other technologies including virtual reality, augmented reality, and the Internet of Things, allowing consumers to connect with technology in new and innovative ways.

6. Expansion of use cases: Chat GPT technology will be

used in a broader number of applications and sectors, including banking, education, and healthcare, resulting in new solutions and possibilities.

Overall, the future of Chat GPT technology seems promising, with the technology predicted to have a substantial influence on a wide range of industries and applications, revolutionizing how we interact with technology and the world around us.

Potential future uses and applications of Chat GPT

There are numerous potential future uses and applications using Chat GPT technology, including:

1. Customer service and support: Chat GPT technology will continue to be utilized to provide instant customer care and assistance via chatbots and virtual assistants.

2. Material creation: Chat GPT technology will be used to produce a wide range of content, including screenplays, plots, and characters for movies, TV shows, and video games.

3. Individualized suggestions: Based on user preferences and behaviors, chat GPT models will be able to deliver highly personalized recommendations for movies, TV series, music, books, and many other types of entertainment.

4. Chat GPT technology will be implemented with e-commerce systems to give quick customer help and product suggestions.

5. Healthcare: Chat GPT technology will be utilized to enhance telemedicine and remote patient monitoring, hence improving patient access to treatment.

6. Education: Chat GPT technology will be utilized to give students real-time tutoring and personalized learning experiences.

7. Financial services: Chat GPT technology will be utilized to give clients financial advice and support, therefore streamlining company operations and improving the end-user experience.

8. Virtual assistants: Chat GPT technology will continue to be integrated into virtual assistants, allowing consumers to connect with technology in more natural and intuitive ways.

9. Chat GPT models will be used to produce news pieces, allowing journalists to focus on more sophisticated and investigative issues.

These are only a few of the numerous potential future uses and applications of Chat GPT technology, and new and novel applications are expected to emerge as this technology develops and becomes increasingly sophisticated.

Discussion on ethical considerations and regulations for the use of Chat GPT technology

Chat GPT technology has raised several ethical considerations and the need for regulations regarding its use. Some of the key ethical considerations include:

1. Bias and prejudice: Because Chat GPT models are trained on vast datasets, they have the potential to accidentally perpetuate existing biases and discrimination in language creation.

2. Privacy and security risks: Chat GPT technology may gather and store vast quantities of personal data, posing concerns about privacy and security.

3. Technology dependence and possible job loss: Chat GPT technology has the potential to automate specific functions and leads to job loss, raising worries about the economic and social impacts.

4. Lack of accountability: Because chat GPT models are taught by algorithms and are not overseen by humans, it is difficult to hold them accountable for their conduct.

In response to these ethical concerns, there have been requests for regulations to be put in place to guarantee that Chat GPT technology is used responsibly. These rules might include data collecting and storage standards, language production openness, AI systems responsibility in language production, and responsibility for AI systems.

Overall, the ethical considerations and regulations surrounding Chat GPT technology are complex and require careful consideration and debate. As the technology continues to advance and become more widespread, these ethical considerations must be addressed, and regulations are put in place to ensure its responsible use.

CHAPTER 7

Conclusion

Summary of key points and takeaways

To summarize, Chat GPT technology has transformed natural language processing and has had a substantial influence on a wide number of industries, including business, healthcare, education, entertainment and media, government, and politics. Greater communication and accessibility, improved customer service and support, optimization of corporate operations, and breakthroughs in education and healthcare are just a few of the primary benefits of Chat GPT technology.

However, there are several possible disadvantages of using Chat GPT technology, including as prejudice and discrimination in language production, a threat to privacy and security, reliance on technology and potential job loss, and challenges in regulating and supervising its usage. These ethical issues underscore the importance of establishing rules and guidelines to ensure the proper use of Chat GPT Technology.

Looking ahead, the future of Chat GPT technology is expected to deliver even more advances and capabilities, as well as possible new uses and applications in a variety of sectors. As this technology matures and becomes more advanced, it is critical to evaluate the ethical issues and rules surrounding its usage to guarantee that its use is responsible and beneficial.

Final thoughts on the impact and significance of Chat GPT in our lives.

Finally, Chat GPT technology has had a significant influence on our lives and has the potential to alter how we communicate, get information, and engage with the world around us. Its capacity to interpret and create natural language has transformed customer service, education, entertainment, and many other sectors.

However, like with any technology, there are worries about its application, such as the possibility of prejudice, discrimination, and privacy infringement. These ethical issues highlight the significance of responsible Chat GPT technology use and development.

Despite these challenges, the importance of Chat GPT in our lives cannot be overestimated. As this technology progresses, it will most certainly play an even greater chunk in molding the future of our society and the way we communicate with one another and the universe around us.

GLOSSARY AND TERMS

1. **Chat GPT:** An advanced language generation model developed by OpenAI that can generate human-like responses to natural language inputs.

2. **Natural language processing (NLP):** The field of artificial intelligence concerned with the interactions between computers and humans using natural language.

3. **Pre-trained:** A machine learning model that has already been trained on a large dataset, allowing it to make predictions on new data without additional training.

4. **Generative model:** A type of machine learning model that can generate new data based on patterns it has learned from existing data.

5. **GPT-3:** The third generation of the Generative Pretrained Transformer language generation model developed by OpenAI.

6. **AI:** Artificial intelligence, a field of computer science focused on creating machines that can perform tasks typically requiring human intelligence, such as understanding language, recognizing patterns, and making decisions.

7. **Neural network:** A type of machine learning model that uses multiple layers of interconnected nodes to process

and analyze data.

8. **Transformer:** A type of neural network architecture specifically designed for processing sequential data, such as text.

9. **API:** Application Programming Interface, a set of rules and protocols for accessing a web-based software application or web tool.

10. **Chatbot:** A computer program designed to simulate conversation with human users, typically through messaging applications, websites, or mobile apps.

11. **Virtual assistant:** A type of chatbot that provides users with personal assistance, such as answering questions, making recommendations, and performing tasks.

12. **Narrow AI:** Artificial intelligence systems that are specifically designed to perform a narrow, well-defined task.

13. **Broad AI:** Artificial intelligence systems that can perform a wide range of tasks and operate more like a human